HEROES OF THE HOLOCAUST

by Rebecca Love Fishkin

Content Adviser:
Harold Marcuse, PhD,
Associate Professor, Department of History,
University of California, Santa Barbara

Reading Adviser:
Alexa Sandmann, EdD,
Professor of Literacy, College and Graduate School
of Education, Health, and Human Services, Kent State University

COMPASS POINT BOOKS
a capstone imprint

Compass Point Books
1710 Roe Crest Drive
North Mankato, MN 56003

Editor: Brenda Haugen
Designer: Ashlee Suker
Media Researcher: Svetlana Zhurkin
Library Consultant: Kathleen Baxter
Production Specialist: Sarah Bennett
Cartographer: XNR Productions, Inc.

On the Cover
Partisan fighters, including the Bielskis, and escapees from the Mir ghetto

Image Credits
Alamy: Chuck Pefley, 55, Eddie Gerald, 56, Steven May, 35; Courtesy of Simon Wiesenthal Center
Library and Archives, Los Angeles, California, 26; Dreamstime/Jorisvo, 9; DVIC/NARA, 31, 59
(all); Getty Images: AFP/Michal Cizek, 17, AFS/Anne Frank House/Anne Frank Fonds, Basel, 40,
Apic, 15; Newscom/AFP/EPA/Pressenbild, 13; United States Holocaust Memorial Museum: courtesy
of Hiroki Sugihara, 21, courtesy of Irving and Emma Eisner, 7, courtesy of Jacqueline Gregory, 54,
courtesy of Jacques Leibman, 6, courtesy of Marion Pritchard, 5, courtesy of Peter Feigl, 53, courtesy
of Rudy Appel, 49, courtesy of Sara Ginaite, 24, courtesy of Shlomo Nadel, 47, courtesy of Vitka
Kempner Kovner, 27, Eric Saul, 22, Eric Saul, courtesy of Dr. Jan Zwartendyk, 20, Frihedsmuseet, 51,
Jack Lennard Archive, Yad Vashem Photo Archives, courtesy of Moshe Kaganovich, cover (detail), 42,
Leopold Page Photographic Collection, 10, 11, Miedzynarodowe Stowarzyszenie im. Janusza Korczaka,
Beit Lohamei Haghetaot, 48, 58, Museum of the Great Patriotic War, 44, National Archives and
Records Administration, Instytut Pamieci Narodowej, 32, Rescuers: Portraits of Moral Courage in
the Holocaust, 36, 38, Yad Vashem, 33, Yad Vashem Photo Archives, Zydowski Instytut Historyczny
imienia Emanuela Ringelbluma, 46.

Library of Congress Cataloging-in-Publication Data
Fishkin, Rebecca Love, 1972–
   Heroes of the Holocaust / by Rebecca Love Fishkin; content adviser,
Harold Marcuse; reading adviser, Alexa Sandmann.
     p. cm.
   "A Capstone imprint."
   Includes bibliographical references and index.
   ISBN 978-0-7565-4391-4 (library binding)
   ISNB 978-0-7565-4443-0 (paperback)
   1. World War, 1939–1945—Jews—Rescue—Juvenile literature. 2. Righteous Gentiles in
the Holocaust—Juvenile literature. 3. World War, 1939–1945—Jewish resistance—Juvenile
literature. 4. Holocaust, Jewish. (1939–1945)—Juvenile literature. I. Title.
   D804.6.F57 2011
   940.53'183—dc22   2010026492

Visit Compass Point Books on the Internet at *www.capstonepub.com*

Printed in the United States of America in North Mankato, Minnesota.
062016   009823R

Table of Contents

Preface

In 1933 an Austrian-born politician named Adolf Hitler became the chancellor of Germany. Hitler was the leader of the National Socialist German Workers Party—the Nazi Party. Hitler was bitterly anti-Semitic and blamed Jews for Germany's economic problems.

Hitler dreamed of populating Europe with Aryans, members of what he called a master race. The Aryans included Germans with fair skin, blond hair, and blue eyes. Hitler believed Jews were the enemy of the Aryans, and he developed a plan to isolate and kill them. Hitler called his plan the Final Solution of the Jewish Question.

With Hitler in power, life for Jews in Germany became increasingly difficult and dangerous. By the mid-1930s, Jewish businesses were boycotted and vandalized. Jewish Germans were forced to identify themselves by wearing the Star of David on their clothing. Jewish children were expelled from German schools. Jews were forced to leave their homes and live in certain areas, apart from Aryans, and they lost their German citizenship. Hitler's police beat and killed some Jews on the streets.

The Nazis sent millions of Jews to concentration camps in many parts of Europe. Some camps were killing centers; others were prison and forced-labor camps. Prisoners were beaten and subjected to painful experiments in which they could be maimed or killed. Survival was rare. Prisoners who were not killed in the gas chambers or shot by guards often died of starvation or illness. Besides Jews, the camps held political prisoners, homosexuals, Jehovah's Witnesses, disabled people, and people who were called gypsies.

Hitler's troops invaded Austria, Czechoslovakia, and Poland, and France and Great Britain declared war on Germany September 3, 1939. World War II became a fight between the Allies—led by France, Great Britain, the United States, and the Soviet Union—and the Axis powers of Germany, Italy, and Japan.

Until their defeat in 1945, the Nazis killed 11 million people in more than a dozen countries. Six million were Jews—two-thirds of the Jewish population in Europe. More than a million Jewish children were killed. This genocide became known as the Holocaust.

CHAPTER 1

There may be times when we are powerless to prevent injustice, but there must never be a time when we fail to protest.

—*Elie Wiesel, Holocaust survivor, author, and Nobel Peace Prize winner*

FIGHTING THE FINAL SOLUTION

Adolf Hitler and the Nazis spread fear and hatred of Jews. Their anti-Jewish propaganda included signs, newspapers, films, books, and public speeches. In schools, books, and youth groups, German children were taught to hate Jews. German citizens were encouraged, and often forced, to treat Jews with cruelty and violence.

Although many gentiles, people who were not Jewish, disagreed with Hitler, resistance was dangerous. A person caught helping a Jew could be jailed, deported, sent to a concentration camp, or even killed immediately.

Still, many German and other European gentiles risked their lives to help Jews. They provided fake papers to help Jews escape to other countries. They built double walls and false ceilings to create hiding spaces in attics, basements, cowsheds, pigeon coops, and latrines. They hid Jews in their homes, churches, offices, and factories. Sometimes the spaces where Jews hid were so small that they could only lie down or crouch for months at a time. The

False papers issued to Chaja Sura Lajbman under the assumed name Helene Yvonne Duviensant

protectors had to lie to their families, neighbors, and the police, and they often had to move Jews from place to place to prevent the Nazis from finding them.

Sandor and Berta Guttman and their nine children in a Budapest safe house

Reasons for Risk

Why did people put themselves and their families at such risk? Gentiles helped for many reasons, including friendship and political opposition to the Nazis. Some helped Jews for financial or personal gain. Others helped because of the known horrors of the concentration camps. Many helped simply because it was the ethical thing to do—to protect other human beings from persecution or danger. Most helped secretly, but some joined large resistance groups.

For Jews, hiding was risky. A Jewish resister could be shot on the spot if discovered. Still, Jews asked gentiles to help them hide.

Jews also took matters into their own hands. They planned uprisings and escapes. They disguised themselves as Aryans. They organized secret schools and religious services, hid Jewish books, and wrote diaries about life and death. The effort to preserve their traditions was a kind of spiritual resistance.

Whether rescuers saved hundreds of Jews or protected just one person or family, these heroes fought the Nazis. Their courage helped stop Hitler from wiping out the European Jewish population.

CHAPTER 2

R. I. P.

✝

OSKAR SCHINDLER

28. 4. 1908 - 9. 10. 1974

ות העולם

> I felt the Jews were being destroyed.
> I had to help them. There was no choice.
>
> —Oskar Schindler, rescuer of 1,200 Jews

DER UNVERGESSLICHE

LEBENRETTER

1200 VERFOLGTER JUDEN

POWERFUL PROTECTION

ot every hero set out to be one. Oskar Schindler was a wealthy, well-connected businessman with a reputation for fine living. A German Catholic with Czechoslovakian citizenship, Schindler worked for the German army and joined the Nazi Party. In 1939 he moved to Krakow, Poland, where he bought a Jewish-owned factory, which became the German Enamel Works. Some of his employees were Jews from the Krakow ghetto. When

Oskar Schindler (second from left) with his Jewish office workers

the Nazis began moving the Krakow Jews to the nearby Plaszów

concentration camp, Schindler started to help his workers.

Using his Nazi connections, Schindler asked favors and bribed

officers to protect the workers from being mistreated at Plaszów or

sent to death camps. He began producing ammunition. That way he

could tell the Nazis that the Jewish workers should be spared because

they were part of the war effort. Schindler also persuaded the Nazis

to let him build a Plaszów subcamp at the German Enamel Works for

1,000 Jewish workers. He brought in 450 more Jewish workers from

nearby factories. Schindler faked records so he could hire workers who were old, disabled, or children. They probably would have been sent to death camps otherwise. Jews in Schindler's camp endured difficult living conditions, but not the brutality and death they would have faced at the hands of the Nazis.

Using His Power

The Nazi Party's ruthless private police force, the Schutzstaffel, usually called the SS, knew Schindler was helping Jews. They arrested him three times, but they could not prove that he was breaking any laws. In 1944 Schindler moved his factory to Brunnlitz,

Jewish laborers built Oskar Schindler's factory in Brunnlitz, Czechoslovakia.

in German-occupied Czechoslovakia. He made a list of 1,200 Jewish prisoners to take with him. The Nazis let him take about 800 men. In addition, a trainload of more than 300 women was sent to the death camp at Auschwitz-Birkenau. But Schindler again used his Nazi connections to rescue the women and bring them to Brunnlitz.

"What I'll say is nothing poetic," said Stella Muller-Madej, one of those rescued by Schindler, "but I will repeat till the end of my days that the first time I was given life [was] by my parents and the second time by Oskar Schindler. In '44 there were around 700 women transported from Płaszów, 300 of whom were on his list, and he fought for us like a lion, because they didn't want to let us out of Auschwitz. He was offered better and healthier 'material' from new [groups of prisoners], unlike us, who had spent several years in the camp. But he got us out. ... He saved us."

Schindler and his wife had become dedicated to helping the Jewish workers survive the war. Their factory was mostly a cover, and it produced very little. Schindler faked production reports and continued to bribe Nazi officials to prevent inspections and deportations.

"We all did very little work," said Murray Pantirer, a man who worked at Schindler's factory. "We always was scared that something gonna happen, that he will be caught, because we did not produce a single piece of ammunition, not a single piece. ... [Schindler] welcomed us, and he said, 'You are [Schindler's Jews] and in here you will survive.'"

Schindler stayed with the Jews in his factory until Soviet troops liberated the Brunnlitz concentration camp on May 9, 1945. He had used all of his wealth to save more than 1,200 Jews, some of whom would later help support him after the war. When Schindler died in 1974, many of the Jews on Schindler's list and their descendants arranged for him to be buried with honor in Israel.

Raoul Wallenberg saved thousands of Jews during World War II.

Saving the Jews of Budapest

In Hungary another well-connected man used his power to protect Jews. Raoul Wallenberg was a Swedish businessman who became a diplomat. In 1944 he was stationed as a diplomat in Budapest, Hungary. Though Hungary was on Germany's side at the start of the war, it later asked for help from the Allies. In response, Germany occupied Hungary and began deporting its Jews to Nazi death camps in Poland. By the time Wallenberg arrived in Budapest, more than 440,000 Hungarian Jews had been sent to the camps. Almost all of them were sent to Auschwitz-Birkenau, the largest extermination camp. About 320,000 were killed upon arrival at the camp.

Wallenberg set out to save the remaining Jews in Budapest. He issued certificates of protection, called Schutz-Passes, from a Swedish diplomatic office. Sweden was a neutral country in the war, and the certificates said the Jews who held the papers were under Swedish protection. He established hospitals and daycare centers for Jews who had certificates. He created more than 30 safe houses that he declared to be Swedish territory. He also employed hundreds of Jews to protect them from deportation.

The Hungarian Arrow Cross, a pro-Nazi group that had seized control of Budapest with Germany's support, realized that many Schutz-Passes were forged and began to deport Jews with fake papers. Asked to identify false certificates, Wallenberg lied as often as possible.

"After we had been standing on line for possibly half a day, we got to the point where we reached Wallenberg and showed him our Schutz-Pass," said Tibor Gonda, a Hungarian Jew. "He had very little time to spend on each case, having to process hundreds and hundreds of them. Obviously we knew that ours was not right, but

SCHUTZ-PASS

Nr. 1/145

Name: Judith Kopstein
Név:

Wohnort: Budapest
Lakás:

Geburtsdatum: 30. Jan 1930
Születési ideje:

Geburtsort: Budapest
Születési helye:

Körperlänge: 171 cm
Magasság:

Haarfarbe: blond Augenfarbe: blau
Hajszín: Szemszín:

Unterschrift: *Judith Kopstein*
Aláírás:

SCHWEDEN

SVÉDORSZÁG

Die Kgl. Schwedische Gesandtschaft in Budapest bestätigt, dass der Obengenannte im Rahmen der — von dem Kgl. Schwedischen Aussenministerium autorisierten — Repatriierung nach Schweden reisen wird. Der Betreffende ist auch in einen Kollektivpass eingetragen.

Bis Abreise steht der Obengenannte und seine Wohnung unter dem Schutz der Kgl. Schwedischen Gesandtschaft in Budapest.

Gültigkeit: erlischt 14 Tage nach Einreise nach Schweden.

A budapesti Svéd Kir. Követség igazolja, hogy fentnevezett — a Svéd Kir. Külügyminisztérium által jóváhagyott — repatriálás keretében Svédországba utazik.

Nevezett a kollektív útlevélben is szerepel.

Elutazásig fentnevezett és lakása a budapesti Svéd Kir. Követség oltalma alatt áll.

Érvényét veszti a Svédországba való megérkezéstől számított tizennegyedik napon.

Raoul Wallenberg saved Judith Kopstein by giving her a Schutz-Pass.

when we got in front of him, he looked at my mother, my sister and me. … He looked at the Schutz-Pass and obviously saw right away that it was forged, but he said, 'This one is OK.' At that moment we were removed from the line, and went to the place where they collected all of those with Wallenberg-approved passes, and there we became human beings again."

The Arrow Cross forced tens of thousands of Jews to walk to Austria. Wallenberg chased them, passing out certificates—real and forged—and then grabbed Jews with certificates out of line to protect them. With the help of other diplomats and the U.S. War Refugee Board, Wallenberg kept tens of thousands of Jews in Budapest alive until the city was liberated in February 1945. Wallenberg was taken to a Soviet prison, probably because the Soviets believed he was a spy for the United States. Wallenberg may have died in prison in 1947. There has never been any confirmation of his death.

Saving the Children

The plight of children during the Holocaust moved many to action. Hitler was eager to kill children to prevent future Jewish generations. Jewish agencies in Great Britain organized an effort called Kindertransport to rescue children from Germany and Austria. About 10,000 children were brought to England, where they lived with foster families and in orphanages for the rest of the war. Most never saw their parents again, because most Jewish families that remained were murdered.

A British stockbroker with a German-Jewish ancestry led a similar effort in Czechoslovakia. Nicholas Winton went to Jewish refugee camps while visiting a friend in Czechoslovakia in 1938. He was horrified by the conditions, especially for the children.

Winton created a Children's Section, modeled after Kindertransport, under the name of the British Committee for Refugees from Czechoslovakia. He collected thousands of applications from Jewish parents, then returned to London to raise the money needed for transportation and to find British families who would care for Czech children. Winton worked hard, keeping his

Nicholas Winton's lifesaving actions during World War II remained a secret for about 50 years. His heroism came to light after his wife found a briefcase with lists of children he had saved and letters from their parents.

day job as a stockbroker and using his late afternoons and evenings to organize the rescue.

"I just left one office and went home and did the other work," he said. "It didn't seem strange to me at the time. ... I don't think when I left the city at three-thirty most of the people knew what I was doing in the evenings."

The first group of child refugees left Prague March 14, 1939. Germany occupied Czechoslovakia the next day.

"We were having supper and sitting around the table and mother was making tea and she suddenly put her knife and fork down and looked at father and she said, 'I heard today that Eva and Vera can go,'" recalled Vera Gissing, a Jew saved by Winton. "I'll never forget the look on father's face. Covered it in his hands. There was a deathly sigh and then he looked up at us and there were tears in his eye. He said, 'Very well, we have to let them hide.'"

Winton arranged seven more transports during the next six months, bringing the children to England by train, then ship. Winton saved at least 669 children before halting rescue efforts when Britain declared war on Germany.

Helping Others Flee

As Allied soldiers fought the Germans on the battlefields, organizations and individuals from around the world joined to fight

Nazi aggression. American journalist Varian Fry was sent to France in the summer of 1940 by the Emergency Rescue Committee, a private American group. He planned to stay one month but remained for more than a year to help political refugees, artists, and scholars whose work opposed the Nazis.

Fry used any means he could to help, including arranging fake papers, using black market supplies and communications, and organizing secret escapes across land and sea. His covert and sometimes illegal methods angered French officials and the U.S. government. He was forced to leave France. Before then, however, he helped about 2,000 refugees flee to safer countries.

An unlikely combination of diplomats from the Netherlands and Japan worked together to rescue Jewish refugees from Lithuania. In 1939 about 15,000 Polish Jews took refuge in Vilnius, Lithuania. Many were highly educated rabbis and students from Mir Yeshiva, a school for studying Jewish texts.

As refugees with no permanent residences or employment, Jews were in danger of deportation when the Soviets occupied Lithuania in 1940. The Soviets closed diplomatic consulates, making it almost impossible to obtain travel visas. But Dutch Ambassador L. P. J. de Decker came up with an idea. He permitted his Lithuanian consul, Jan Zwartendijk, to give Jews false papers saying they could enter the Dutch Caribbean island of Curaçao without visas. The papers gave them a destination for escape.

To leave Lithuania, Jews needed travel visas that would let them cross the Pacific Ocean. The solution came from Japan's consul in Lithuania, Chiune Sempo Sugihara. He issued visas to 2,140 Jews to allow them to travel through Japan. Though forbidden to do so by Tokyo, Sugihara even issued visas to people who had no final destinations or travel money. He knew the Soviets would honor the Japanese visas, and he hoped the Jews would be able to secure authentic

For his heroism during World War II, Jan Zwartendijk was named Righteous Among Nations by Israel's Holocaust Martyrs' and Heroes' Remembrance Authority.

travel permits to go to other countries once out of Europe.

"My sister and I pushed ourselves into the room with Mr. Sugihara," said former Jewish refugee Lucille Szepsenwol Camhi. "He asked us our name. He asked us where our parents were. We told him. My father was not living. My mother has no papers. And he looked very sympathetic at us and he just stamped, gave us the visa right there on the spot."

Jews traveled by the Trans-Siberian railroad from Vilnius to

Chiune Sempo Sugihara asked his government three times for permission to issue visas to Jewish refugees. Each time he was refused. He decided to issue them anyway.

the Russian coastal port of Vladivostok. The Soviets prevented a few from leaving the country, but most boarded Japanese ships for a voyage with an unknown end.

"As we crossed the sea towards Japan, we waited in quiet anxiety for the day when we should pass beyond Russian territorial waters," said Oskar Schenker, who fled Vilnius with a Japanese visa. "It came at last. The red flag was lowered and the Soviet officials left the ship. Freedom lay ahead. Japan was to be for us really the land of the rising sun."

When they arrived in Japan with little money and few possessions, the Jews tried to obtain visas to continue their journeys. Some obtained visas to travel to the United States and other safe countries, but about half were sent to Shanghai, China, which was occupied by Japan. There they joined more than 20,000 Russian, German, and Austrian Jewish refugees who had fled to Japan earlier in the war.

Jewish refugees escaped to Canada from Europe with Japanese transit visas issued by Chiune Sugihara in Kaunas, Lithuania.

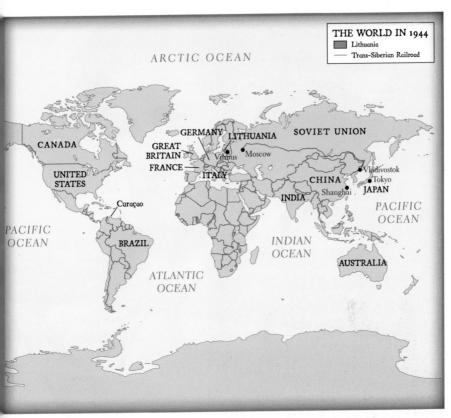

THE WORLD IN 1944
- Lithuania
— Trans-Siberian Railroad

ARCTIC OCEAN

CANADA

GREAT
BRITAIN
FRANCE

GERMANY
LITHUANIA
Vilnius
Moscow

SOVIET UNION

ITALY

UNITED
STATES

Curaçao

CHINA
Shanghai

Vladivostok
Tokyo
JAPAN

INDIA

PACIFIC
OCEAN

PACIFIC
OCEAN

BRAZIL

INDIAN
OCEAN

AUSTRALIA

ATLANTIC
OCEAN

Jewish refugees from Lithuania traveled across Asia to Japan, where some boarded ships bound for the United States, Canada, or other countries that offered them safety.

The Jews lived in a ghetto in Shanghai. Conditions were poor, and they lived with restrictions, but they did not have the daily fear they had faced in Europe. They maintained a strong sense of Jewish community, building a synagogue and creating newspapers, poems, art, and plays. The Polish students and rabbis from Vilnius continued their studies, forming the only eastern European yeshiva to survive the Holocaust. The Jews in Shanghai did not learn of the devastation of the Holocaust until the end of the war.

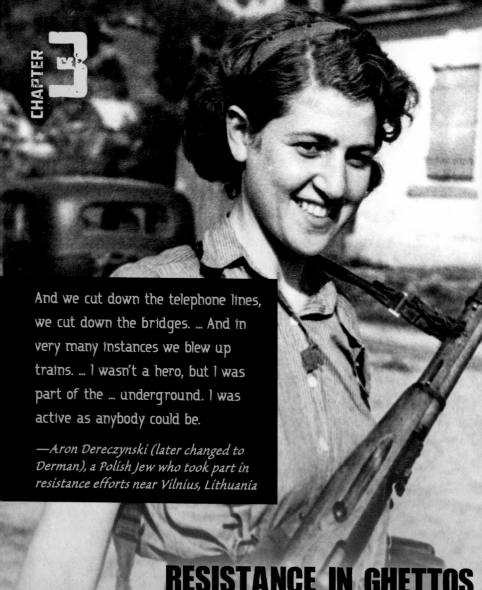

CHAPTER 3

And we cut down the telephone lines, we cut down the bridges. ... And in very many instances we blew up trains. ... I wasn't a hero, but I was part of the ... underground. I was active as anybody could be.

—Aron Dereczynski (later changed to Derman), a Polish Jew who took part in resistance efforts near Vilnius, Lithuania

RESISTANCE IN GHETTOS AND CONCENTRATION CAMPS

The Nazis took away Jewish property and forced hundreds of thousands of Jews to live in ghettos to isolate them from non-Jews. The ghettos were crowded and dirty. Many Jews in them died from disease or starvation.

"The hunger in the ghetto was so great, was so bad, that people were lying on the streets and dying, little children went around begging, and ... every day you walked out in the morning, you see somebody is lying dead, covered with newspapers or with any kind of blanket they found," said Abraham Lewent, a Warsaw ghetto survivor. "And every day thousands and thousands died just from malnutrition because the Germans didn't give anything for the people in the ghetto to eat."

Keeping the Faith

Despite all of the hardships, the spirit of survival was strong in the ghettos. The Jews valued education and religious community, and they did all they could to preserve them. In the Vilnius ghetto in Lithuania, Jews organized schools, plays, and secret holiday celebrations. They published newspapers, created art, and wrote poetry. They also hid a vast library of Jewish books.

Yitskhok Rudashevski was a Jewish boy born in Vilnius in 1927. His father worked for a newspaper, and his mother was a seamstress. Rudashevski valued his education and was intent on continuing his studies even after his family was forced into the Vilnius ghetto with 55,000 other Jews.

Rudashevski joined a peaceful resistance effort to collect ghetto history. He interviewed other residents about their property, families, hideouts, jokes, and songs, and other details of ghetto life. He wrote everything down so no one would forget this part of Jewish history. Rudashevski also belonged to a youth club that performed plays, gave concerts, and offered poetry readings.

"Today we had a club holiday in the kitchen," Rudashevski wrote in his diary December 11, 1942. "We felt like having a little fun. So we wangled a hundred kilograms of

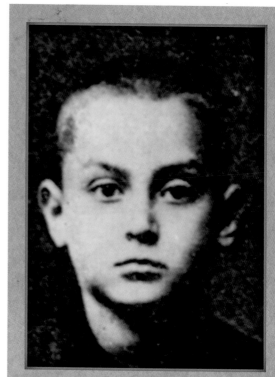

Yitskhok Rudashevski likely died in the fall of 1943, but his cousin found his diary. It was published in 1973.

potatoes out of the administration and we have a baked pudding. This was the happiest evening I have spent in the ghetto. ... [Club] members came with songs, recitations. Until late into the night we sang with the adults songs that tell about youthfulness and hope. ... Today we have demonstrated that even within the three small streets we can maintain our youthful zeal. We have proved that from the ghetto there will not emerge a youth broken in spirit; from the ghetto there will emerge a strong youth which is hardy and cheerful."

Revolt in Ghettos and Camps

Jewish youth played important roles in cultural and violent ghetto resistance. One of them in Vilnius was 23-year-old Abba Kovner, a leader of the United Organization of Partisans (UOP). Kovner suspected the Nazis would eventually move the Vilnius Jews to concentration camps, so he organized a revolt.

Abba Kovner in Vilnius after the Soviet army forced out the Germans in 1944

"Hitler is plotting to destroy all European Jews," Kovner told Jewish youth in a speech December 31, 1941. "[Lithuania's] Jews will be the first in line. Let us not be led like sheep to the slaughterhouse. It is right, we are weak and without defense, but the only answer to the enemy is resistance!"

The UOP gathered weapons through the black market and planned ways to resist the Germans. When the Nazis decided to send the Vilnius Jews to concentration camps, the UOP fought back. On September 1, 1943, they shot at German guards, who then blew up buildings in the ghetto in retaliation.

UOP members escaped through the sewers. Many were caught and killed, but those who survived outside the ghetto, including Kovner, fought from hideouts in the forest for the rest of the war. They sabotaged German water and power supplies and blew up military trains. They freed prisoners from work camps and persuaded Jews in other ghettos to rebel. Similar groups of underground fighters carried on such activities across Europe. Their efforts rarely had large-scale results, but they gave hope to Jews everywhere.

In the Warsaw ghetto—where as many as 400,000 people lived in overcrowded conditions—fear, sickness, and starvation were rampant. Jews and gentiles, inside and outside the Polish ghetto, worked to smuggle food and medicines into the ghetto and sneak children out. But rumors circulated that the Nazis would soon deport the Jews to work and death camps.

The Germans had created a Jewish administration, the Judenrat, which was forced to carry out Nazi orders of brutality in the ghettos. The leader of the Warsaw ghetto Judenrat was Adam Czerniakow. He struggled to help his fellow Jews, using the power of his position to help keep secrets from the Germans and to ease the punishments he was ordered to inflict.

On July 22, 1942, the Nazis began a massive deportation of

Even though they were confined to ghettos, Jews continued to offer resistance against the Nazis.

Jews to concentration camps. Czerniakow was ordered to help with the deportation. He tried to get exemption papers for as many Jews as possible and begged for orphaned children to remain in Warsaw. His requests were denied. Rather than help lead his people to death, Czerniakow committed suicide. His diary survived the war and provides important details of life inside the ghetto.

About 300,000 Jews from the Warsaw ghetto were killed or deported, mostly to the Treblinka extermination camp in Poland, from July 22 to September 12. The remaining 60,000 Jews knew it would only be a matter of time before they too would be sent to the camps. They decided to fight.

Inside the ghetto leaders of various Jewish resistance groups united to create the Jewish Combat Organization. With help from the Polish Home Army, an underground resistance effort, they collected firearms and explosives. When the Germans came to deport the remaining Jews on January 18, 1943, the Jews shot at the police, holding them off for three days. Many of the Jewish fighters were killed during the Warsaw ghetto uprising, but their efforts gave Jews in the ghetto time to hide. The Germans deported only about 5,000 to 6,500 Jews instead of the whole ghetto. The fighters built more underground bunkers and gathered weapons for the next fight.

On April 19, 1943, the Germans returned. The ghetto appeared empty at first. With most of the ghetto population safe in the

Some members of the Jewish resistance were captured by SS troops during the Warsaw ghetto uprising.

bunkers, the armed resistance forced the Nazis to retreat outside the walls and killed dozens of German soldiers. After about two days of fighting, the Germans began tearing the ghetto to the ground, house by house. The Jews hid or fought for almost a month until nearly all had been killed or captured and sent to extermination camps. Although only a few survivors were able to escape through the sewers, the fight inspired uprisings in other ghettos and camps.

"Something happened beyond our wildest dreams: the Germans twice ran away from the ghetto. One of our units held out 40 minutes, another more than six hours," Mordechai Anielewicz, a Warsaw ghetto resistance leader, wrote April 23 to a friend outside the ghetto.

SS troops searched ruined buildings for survivors during the Warsaw ghetto uprising.

"Many fires in the ghetto. Yesterday the hospital was burning. Whole blocks of houses are on fire. ... I cannot describe to you the conditions under which Jews live. Only exceptional individuals will survive. The rest will die, sooner or later. Their fate is sealed. ... What's most important: the dream of my life has become a reality. I lived to see Jewish defense in the ghetto in all its greatness and splendor."

Revolt in the camps was more difficult. The Nazis built about 20,000 camps across Europe to imprison Jews. Prisoners were beaten, starved, and tortured. Disease was rampant. Families were ripped apart. Hundreds of thousands of people were killed in gas chambers upon arrival. Their bodies were cremated in ovens, dumped into mass graves, or burned in huge piles.

Witnessing these horrors, Jewish prisoners in many camps staged uprisings and escapes. Jews at the Treblinka extermination

wish women selected for forced labor at Auschwitz-Birkenau marched toward their arracks carrying bedrolls after disinfection and headshaving.

camp, armed with stolen weapons, set fire to a gas chamber August 2, 1943. They planned to escape and join a group of Jews who were hiding in the forest. The prisoners killed several guards. More than 300 prisoners escaped, but about 100 were later caught and killed. The camp was shut down after the uprising.

At the Sobibor camp, prisoners set a fire and killed 11 guards October 14, 1943. About 300 prisoners tried to escape through a surrounding minefield. More than 100 were caught and shot, and many were killed by mines. Two days later the Nazis ordered the camp's destruction.

Several attempts at rebellion occurred at Auschwitz-Birkenau. In one effort, plans were made to blow up a crematorium. Jewish prisoner Rosa Robota and about 20 other women smuggled in gunpowder and explosives. The prisoners made bombs and hid them around the camp. On October 7, 1944, after learning that they were scheduled to be killed, Jewish workers blew up a crematorium and gas chamber, and they killed several guards. The Nazis found those involved and killed them, including Robota.

Although camp uprisings saved few lives, the efforts inspired many Jews to keep fighting and boosted their hope that somehow they would survive the war.

I'm always happy when I think about that horrible time, that occupation of our country, that I could help, that I had the possibility. Every day. And I'm very thankful for the way that God helped us.

—Johtje Vos, who sheltered 30 Dutch Jews

CHAPTER 4

Monument to Janusz Korczak

ORDINARY PEOPLE, EXTRAORDINARY EFFORTS

Through diaries, photographs, letters, and books, Holocaust survivors

have told the stories of courageous gentiles and Jews who saved their

lives. Some heroes helped one person or a family. Some saved dozens.

Others organized efforts that helped thousands.

Jews hid behind walls, in cupboards, and under floors. They took refuge in

churches, hospitals, forests, and zoos. Children were smuggled out of ghettos in coffins, laundry bags, and potato sacks. They escaped to safer countries in ambulances, on fishing boats, and by foot. They were helped by friends, business acquaintances, and strangers. The heroes were housewives, nurses, teachers, priests, farmers, and police— everyday people who risked their lives to help.

Dutch Efforts

Resistance was widespread in the Netherlands. An anti-German underground movement helped forge documents and ration cards and found Jews safe places to hide.

Bert and Annie Bochove ran a drugstore in Huizen, near

Annie and Bert Bochove, photographed with their children, Eric and Marise, risked their lives to hide many Jews during the war.

Amsterdam. They opposed the Nazis but lived quietly until the summer of 1942, when a Jewish friend, Henny Juliard, came to them for help. The Bochoves hid Juliard, her husband, and her sister above their drugstore. Bert Bochove's brothers asked him to help another family, the Rodrigueses, who were Portuguese Jews.

Bert built a hiding place in the attic of their home. Its entrance was a secret door that was hidden by shelves stocked with pharmacy goods. They put paper inside the attic walls so they would sound like regular walls if knocked upon. Slowly, more Jews asked for help, and the Bochoves took in many more people than could fit comfortably in the house.

"After the Juliards and the Rodrigues family, it was all unknown people coming into my house," Bert Bochove said. "There was a network in the underground that brought people to us: I didn't understand how it worked, and was never interested either. After all, with so many strangers coming into my house, the less I knew the better. Sometimes it wasn't until years later that I knew their real names; with some, I never learned them."

A clerk they hired to help in the drugstore betrayed the Bochoves by telling her German boyfriend about the hidden Jews. A trusted friend hid some of the Jews, and the Bochoves posted a fake quarantine sign on the door to keep out the Germans. The Bochoves and the Jews survived the betrayal, as well as future

The balcony built by Bert Bochove, adjacent to the attic where he hid 37 Jews during World War II

German searches, but they had to be alert at all times. Food was scarce and quarters were tight. Nevertheless, by the end of the war, they had hidden 37 Jews, including several children.

In the nearby town of Laren, Johtje and Aart Vos hid more than 30 Dutch Jews. The Voses had Jewish friends and hated the Nazis. They offered to take in a child from friends who faced deportation. One day, another couple—who the Voses had not known were Jewish—asked the Voses to keep a suitcase full of valuables while they fled. Soon they were taking in more Jews, including more children. They covered the floor with mattresses, lied to the Gestapo political police, and developed signals to tell Jews when it was safe to approach.

"You were not allowed to have Jewish people in your house,

visiting or living. ... We started immediately to be very active to help the Jewish people so that included a lot of fear, of course, and danger, so our life changed very much," Johtje Vos said. "They were in need of help. It's like when you see a child fall in the water, you jump in and get him out."

A Dutch police officer developed a code to let the Voses know when Nazis were coming. He would call their phone, let it ring twice, hang up, and then repeat the steps. When they got the signal, Jews in the Vos home would go through a trap door in a shed that led to a tunnel. They would crawl to the forest and hide until the Voses told them it was safe. The Voses and the Jews they hid survived the war.

Perhaps the most famous story of resistance in the Netherlands is that of Anne Frank, a Dutch teenager who spent two years in hiding with her sister, parents, and four other Jews. They were protected and cared for by a small group of friends: Johannes Kleiman, Victor Kugler, Bep and Johan Voskuijl, and Jan and Miep Gies.

Born in Austria as Hermine Santruschitz, Miep Gies went to the Netherlands as part of a post-World War I program that placed sick or weak children with Dutch families to recover. She stayed with her foster family for five years, never returning to Austria. She married Jan Gies in 1941 and became a Dutch citizen. She worked as a secretary for Otto Frank, Anne's father.

In June 1942 Anne's sister, Margot, was summoned for work duty by the Germans. Her father decided it was time to hide. He had planned for the possibility, asking the Gieses and the others to help. The Gieses moved clothing and supplies to a secret annex above Otto's office. On July 6 the Franks went into hiding. They were joined by Hermann and Auguste van Pels and their son, Peter, and a dentist, Fritz Pfeffer. For two years, Gies and the others kept the hiding place a secret, providing the hidden Jews with everything they needed for survival.

"Miep and [Bep] had the extremely difficult task to provide food. To nourish 8 people while most of the food-stuff was rationed, was a hard job," Otto Frank wrote in a letter in 1971. "They had to buy in different shops, so that it would not raise suspicion if they bought big quantities in one. Mr. Gies and Mr. Kleiman bought ration-cards on

Miep and Jan Geis on their wedding day, July 16, 1941

the black market for us and when after some time we became short of money, they sold parts of our jewellry. … Every day our helpers came to see us. … Their moral support was very important for us. They gave us an optimistic view on the situation if possible and tried to conceal bad news. There was much tension in their lives during these two years."

On August 4, 1944, Germans burst into the office and found the Jews. All were arrested and sent to concentration camps. Miep Gies was in the office at the time. Because she had been born in Austria, one of the Nazi officers, who was also Austrian, did not arrest her. They did not know that Gies and her husband also were hiding an anti-Nazi Dutch student in their home. Jan Gies also escaped arrest, but the other protectors were taken away.

After the arrest, Miep Gies found Anne Frank's diary pages and notebooks and hid them. She kept them, unread, and gave them to Otto Frank at the end of the war. He was the only Jew from the secret annex who survived. Anne Frank died in the Bergen-Belsen camp less than two months before liberation.

"I am not a hero," Miep Gies said. "I stand at the end of the long, long line of good Dutch people who did what I did and more— much more—during those dark and terrible times years ago, but always like yesterday in the heart of those of us who bear witness."

Resistance Elsewhere

Some resistance efforts saved thousands of lives. In Belarus, in the
Nazi-occupied part of the Soviet Union, three brothers lost their
parents and siblings when the Nazis killed and deported Jews from
their town. Tuvia, Aleksander—known as Zus—and Asael Bielski
escaped and became leaders of a Jewish resistance movement.
They hid in the forest and recruited other Jews to help fight the
Nazis. From 1942 to 1944, about 1,200 Jews, including women and
children, were with them.

At first the Bielski group moved constantly to hide from
German police. By the end of 1943, however, they had established

Partisans from various fighting units, including the Bielski group, and escapees from the
Mir ghetto guarded an airstrip in the Naliboki forest in the Soviet Union in 1944.

a permanent base in the forest. They built a bakery, a synagogue, a medical clinic, a school, a jail, and a theater. The Jews used their skills as doctors, cooks, carpenters, tailors, teachers, and more to create a community.

The Bielski fighters used sabotage against the Germans, killed some, and freed Jews from ghettos. They blew up train tracks and bridges. They formed an alliance with Soviet resistance fighters who also were battling the Germans. More than 1,000 members of the Bielski community, including the brothers, survived the Holocaust.

"The doors from the [Bielski brothers] were open for everybody, for old, children, sick people. And they [always had] food. They didn't have steaks, but they have bread and water," said Sonia Boldo Bielski, Aleksander Bielski's wife. "This was the life. We were fighting them not in the open. You cannot fight a German soldier in the open. We were surrounding them. We know where they are and we were fighting them and took off everything from them."

Resistance also helped save Jews by giving them a reason to keep fighting when they thought all hope was gone. One inspiring resister was Faye Lazebnik Schulman, who was born an Orthodox Jew in Lenin, Poland. She was educated and learned four languages. At 16 she took over her family's photography business. The Nazis invaded Lenin in 1941, sending some of Schulman's family to a ghetto. Schulman's brothers were sent to labor camps. When the

Nazis killed the Jews in the ghetto, Schulman was spared because the Germans wanted to use her photography skills.

The Nazis made Schulman take and develop pictures of the ghetto. She kept secret copies, so she could later prove all of the horrors of ghetto life. One photo showed the mass grave where the Nazis had buried members of her family. When Jewish partisans attacked the town, Schulman escaped and joined the resistance. She learned to shoot a gun and to care for the wounded. She stole food, medicine, and weapons. She also took photographs to document all of the partisans' actions.

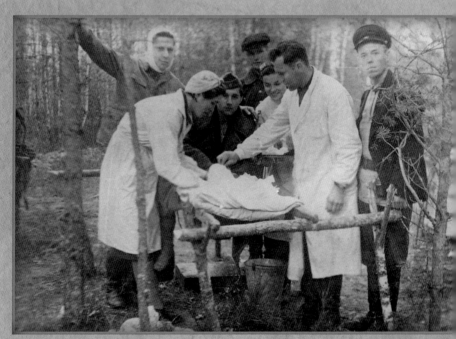

A wounded partisan was treated at a field hospital. Faye Lazebnik Schulman (left) was a photographer and partisan nurse.

"This was the only way I could fight back and revenge my family," she said. "When it was time to be hugging a boyfriend, I was hugging a rifle. Now I said to myself, my life is changed. I learned how to look after the wounded. I even learned how to make operations."

Schulman survived the war and became a newspaper photographer in Russia. In 1945 she was reunited with a brother who had escaped the Nazis and joined a partisan group. She married another resistance fighter, Morris Schulman, and eventually moved to Canada.

Risking Everything for Jewish Youth

Many people risked their lives to help Jewish children. Irena Sendler, a Catholic social worker in Warsaw, Poland, provided clothing, money, and medicine for Jews who registered under false names. With Sendler's help, Jews pretended to have contagious illnesses, which prevented inspection by the Nazis.

Sendler was part of an underground resistance group called Zegota (Council for Aid to Jews). Because she was a social worker, Sendler could enter the Warsaw ghetto daily to take in medicine and food. With starvation and disease killing thousands of ghetto residents each month, Sendler decided to try to rescue at least some of the children.

Sendler had to persuade Jewish parents to let their children be cared for outside the ghetto by non-Jewish families. Finding willing parents was difficult. If the Nazis found out, the children and their caregivers would be killed. Sendler smuggled out some children by ambulance. They were often hidden in potato sacks and coffins.

Sometimes using fake documents and forged signatures supplied by a network of helpers,

Irena Sendler headed the children's section of Zegota.

Sendler rescued 2,500 children. She gave them non-Jewish identities and took them to homes, convents, and orphanages. She kept secret notes about every child to help them find their parents after the war. She made a list of their real names and put it in a jar that she buried in a neighbor's backyard.

"Every child saved with my help and the help of all the wonderful secret messengers, who today are no longer living, is the justification of my existence on this earth, and not a title to glory," Sendler said.

The children never knew her real name, but the Nazis discovered Sendler's activities and arrested her in 1943. She was tortured and imprisoned, but she kept the names of the children a secret. Zegota members freed her from prison before she could be executed, and she continued her work in secret. After the war she dug up the jar, but many of the children's parents had been killed. In 2000 high school students in Kansas created a play about Sendler's heroism, titled *Life in a Jar*. It has been performed around the world. Sendler was nominated for a Nobel Peace Prize in 2007 and died in 2008.

In the Warsaw ghetto, another hero fought for Jewish children, but this story did not end in survival. When war broke out in Poland, Janusz Korczak was running an orphanage. Born Henryk

Children from the Korczak orphanage

Goldsmit, Korczak was a doctor and author. He had always helped children, befriending youths in poor neighborhoods, then becoming an orphanage director and publishing a children's newspaper. He published fiction and nonfiction books about children and created a Jewish orphanage that promoted education.

Janusz Korczak's orphanage took in children from 7 to 14 years old.

When the Germans forced Jews into the Warsaw ghetto, the orphanage moved inside too. Many friends offered to hide Korczak, but he refused to leave the orphans. In August 1942 the Germans were going to send Korczak and about 200 orphans to an extermination camp. Korczak again refused to hide. He did not want the children to go to the camp alone. He dressed them in their best clothes and held a child's hand as the Germans marched them to a train. They were all murdered at Treblinka. Korczak's bravery and dedication to the children, however, lives on as an example of Jews' refusal to let the Nazis destroy their spirit.

CHAPTER 5

LE CHAMBON SUR LIGNON
0 K 85

obody asked who was Jewish and who was not. Nobody
sked where you were from. Nobody asked who your
ather was or if you could pay. They just accepted each
f us, taking us in with warmth, sheltering children,
ften without their parents—children who cried in the
ight from nightmares.

—Elizabeth Koenig-Kaufman, a former child refugee in
e Chambon-sur-Lignon, France

Dr. Juliette Usaach cared for Jewish children in
Le Chambon-sur-Lignon

SAFE HAVENS

Before World War II began, a few nations took in Jewish refugees who

were fleeing the growing threat of the Nazis. Once the war began,

however, even those nations enacted stricter immigration laws or

stopped admitting refugees. As the Germans occupied more European nations,

many countries that had been sympathetic to Jewish refugees simply watched

as they were sent to concentration camps. An exception was Denmark, which became the only occupied country to devote itself to saving its Jewish citizens.

When the Nazis occupied Denmark in 1940, they found the country's 7,500 Jewish residents living in harmony with most non-Jewish Danes. Denmark's King Christian X strongly supported Jewish Danes. At first the Germans let the Danish government control the treatment of Jews. They did not have to register property, leave their homes, or wear identification badges. Jews lived and worked among non-Jews and held religious services.

That lenient policy ended in 1943, when the Germans decided to deport Danish Jews to concentration camps. A few German officials told non-Jewish Danes about the coming deportation. Those Danes warned the Jewish community. In a huge protection effort, Danish authorities and citizens hid their Jewish neighbors in homes, churches, and hospitals. When the deportation began, Danish police prevented Germans from entering Jewish homes by force. Only a handful of Jews were found.

Danish resistance workers helped Jews move secretly to the coast, where fishermen took them to safety in Sweden. In one month about 7,200 Jews and about 700 of their non-Jewish family members became refugees, leaving their homes for Sweden.

"We hid them in houses near the shore and brought them to waiting boats at an appointed time," explained Preben Munch-Nielsen,

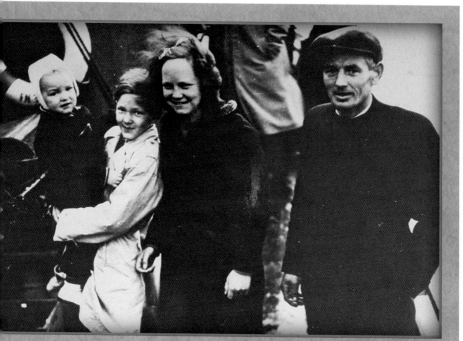

ewish refugees were ferried out of Denmark on fishing boats bound for Sweden.

who ferried Jews to Sweden. "Under cover of darkness, we took up to 12 Jews at a time across the straits to Sweden."

The Germans did deport about 470 Jews to a ghetto in Czechoslovakia, but the Danish government and the Red Cross insisted on being told the Jews' location and living conditions. That is probably why the Germans didn't move the Danish Jews to death camps. Only about 120 Danish Jews were killed during the Holocaust, giving Denmark one of the highest survival rates of German-occupied European countries. When the surviving Jews returned to Denmark, most found that their homes and businesses had been protected by neighbors and Danish authorities. In most other German-occupied countries, property left behind by Jewish refugees was confiscated or destroyed.

French Protection

Until 1939, when the German threat could no longer be ignored, France was a safe haven for Jews. The Allied nation admitted many refugees, including non-Jewish anti-Nazi activists. The German occupation changed everything for the 350,000 Jews living in France. New laws prevented them from serving in the civil service or the army. They were no longer allowed to practice medicine or law or to teach. Many Jews were sent to concentration camps.

One small area of France remained a sanctuary. Le Chambon-sur-Lignon was a village in the hills of south-central France. The residents opposed Hitler and were sympathetic to Jews. When their Protestant Huguenot pastor, André Trocmé, asked the villagers and those from nearby towns to help shelter Jews, they agreed.

Efforts began in 1940, when Trocmé started helping Jews held in nearby concentration camps. He offered to hide the children in homes in his village. With the help of the children's rescue group Oeuvre de Secours aux Enfants (OSE), the children were taken to Le Chambon-sur-Lignon and surrounding villages. The Swiss Red Cross, the Quakers, American Congregationalists, and even some national governments provided money for some children's homes;

The French village of Le Chambon-sur-Lignon as it looked in 1940

others lived in private homes. The Jewish children had false papers and pretended to be Christian villagers.

"A social worker from the OSE came to see my mother and explained that there was a village ... Le Chambon ... [that] was looking to help young people, to take them out of the camp and would she agree to let me go. ... She let me go. She loved me enough to let me go," said Hanne Hirsch Liebmann. "And Le Chambon was, of course, heaven. We were free."

Jewish adults also sought shelter in the villages. Trocmé, with the help of his wife, Magda, and assistant, Edouard Theis, forged documents and sneaked Jews across the border to Switzerland. Though the villagers had little food or money, they shared their homes, moving the refugees around to keep them hidden from German inspectors. Everyone kept the secret. French police arrested Trocmé and Theis and held them in a camp for about a month. Magda Trocmé eventually took over the rescue efforts when her husband and Theis were forced into hiding. Even with the threat of arrest and punishment, the villagers continued to offer protection. No Jew was ever turned away. The residents of Le Chambon-sur-Lignon, with the help of people from other communities, saved 3,000 to 5,000 Jews and anti-Nazi activists.

"These people came here for help and for shelter," said André Trocmé. "I am their shepherd. A shepherd does not forsake his flock. … I do not know what a Jew is. I know only human beings."

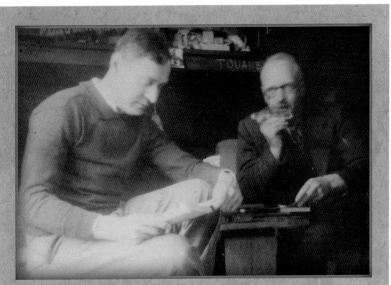

Edouard Theis (left) and André Trocmé during their imprisonment at a French camp

e who saves a single soul,

aves the world entire.

—Inscription on a ring given to Oskar

chindler by the Jews of Brunnlitz

REMEMBERING THE HEROES

Hundreds of accounts of resistance, rescue, and survival have been documented since the Holocaust. Millions of Jews and non-Jews learn these stories by visiting museums and memorials around the world.

The United States Holocaust Memorial Museum in Washington, D.C., opened in 1993. Exhibits include letters, diaries, newspapers, and photographs that tell the stories of Holocaust survivors, victims, rescuers, and Nazis. The museum has a vast library, an extensive website, and a special section on children.

Yad Vashem began in 1953 as "the Jewish people's living memorial to the Holocaust." Located in Jerusalem, Israel, Yad Vashem conducts research and provides education worldwide. One of its important activities is recognizing the people who helped Jews during the Holocaust. Yad Vashem created the Righteous Among the Nations program to award certificates of honor and medals. Many of the heroes in this book have been recognized as Righteous

Yad Vashem's Hall of Remembrance with the names of World War II death camps

Among the Nations. Their names are listed in Yad Vashem's Hall of Remembrance, and trees honoring especially brave rescuers are planted along the approaching road. Survivors, as well as families and friends, can contact Yad Vashem to nominate someone for recognition.

After the war many countries turned Nazi concentration camps into museums and memorials to the victims. Dachau in Germany and Auschwitz-Birkenau in Poland are two examples. Their grounds are open to the public. Visitors can see photos, artifacts, and videos of life in the camps.

Work Continues

The effort to help the Jews of the Holocaust continues today. Many people, including government officials and lawyers, are helping Jews recover property taken by the Nazis. Others are helping Jews trace the events of the war to find out what happened to their families. Historians research stories of survival and resistance, and educators teach new generations of students about the Holocaust.

The Jews who survived the Holocaust and the heroes who helped many people survive are now old or have died, but their courage lives on. They are leaving behind lessons about the power of both hatred and compassion. And they are spreading hope that new heroes will step forward wherever persecution and genocide arise.

**December 1, 1938–
September 1, 1939**

British Kindertransport
rescues 9,000 to
10,000 children

Nicholas Winton
transports Czech
children to England

**March 14, 1939–
August 2, 1939**

Germany invades
Poland, and World
War II begins

Miep Gies and others
hide Anne Frank and
her family in Amsterdam

**July 6, 1942–
August 4, 1944**

August 1942

Janusz Korczak
accompanies the
children of his orphanage
to the Treblinka
extermination camp,
where all are murdered

Oskar Schindler
moves his factory and
1,200 Jewish workers
to Brunnlitz

October 14, 1943

Uprising at
Sobibor camp

October 1944

April 15, 1945

British troops liberate
Bergen-Belsen

Timeline

Villagers of Le Chambon-sur-Lignon in France, with help from people in other villages, shelter Jews

December 1940–September 1944

January 1941

Refugees from Vilnius, Lithuania, arrive in Japan with Curaçao visas

Bielski partisans fight and hide in forests of Belarus

1942-1944

Warsaw ghetto uprising

April 19-May 16, 1943

August 2, 1943

Uprising at Treblinka

Vilnius ghetto partisans shoot German police

September 1, 1943

Prisoners at Auschwitz-Birkenau camp blow up a crematorium

October 6, 1944

May 8, 1945

Germany surrenders, ending the war in Europe

Glossary

aggression—forceful action, sometimes without a reasonable cause

anti-Semitism—prejudice or discrimination against Jewish people

concentration camp—prison camp built by Nazis to hold Jews and others, including communists and anti-Nazi political activists, Jehovah's Witnesses, homosexuals, some criminals, and those they called gypsies

covert—secret

deportation—sending someone out of a country

ethical—following accepted rules of behavior

Final Solution—Adolf Hitler's plan to eliminate all European Jews

genocide—systematic mass murder of a national, racial, religious, or ethnic group

gentiles—non-Jews

latrines—pits in the earth used as toilets

liberated—set free

partisan—member of a group of fighters that attacks and harasses an enemy

propaganda—information spread to try to influence the thinking of people; often not completely true or fair

refugees—people who are forced to leave their homes because of persecution, war, or natural disaster

Star of David—six-pointed star that is a symbol of Judaism

visa—document that permits a citizen of one country to travel to and from another country

yeshiva—school for the study of Jewish holy writings

Additional Resources

Further Reading

Burgan, Michael. *Refusing to Crumble: The Danish Resistance in World War II*. Minneapolis: Compass Point Books, 2010.

Frank, Anne. *The Diary of a Young Girl*. New York: Alfred A. Knopf, 2010.

Haugen, Brenda. *Adolf Hitler: Dictator of Nazi Germany*. Minneapolis: Compass Point Books, 2006.

Haugen, Brenda. *The Holocaust Museum*. Minneapolis: Compass Point Books, 2008.

Hill, Jeff. *The Holocaust*. Detroit: Omnigraphics, 2006.

Klempner, Mark. *The Heart Has Reasons: Holocaust Rescuers and Their Stories of Courage*. Cleveland: Pilgrim Press, 2006.

Wood, Angela Gluck. *Holocaust: The Events and Their Impact on Real People*. New York: DK Publishing, 2007.

Internet Sites

Use FactHound to find Internet sites related to this book. All of the sites on FactHound have been researched by our staff.

Here's all you do:
Visit *www.facthound.com*
Type in this code: 9780756543914

Select Bibliography

Bloom, Harold, ed. *Anne Frank's The Diary of Anne Frank*. New York: Bloom's Literary Criticism, 2010.

Grynberg, Michal, ed. *Words to Outlive Us: Voices from the Warsaw Ghetto*. New York: Metropolitan Books, 1988.

Holliday, Laurel. *Children in the Holocaust and World War II: Their Secret Diaries*. New York: Pocket Books, 1995.

Holocaust Education & Archive Research Team. "Oskar Schindler." 29 July 2010. www.holocaustresearchproject.org/survivor/schindler.html

Jewish Virtual Libary. "Janusz Korczak." 29 July 2010. www.jewishvirtuallibrary.org/jsource/biography/Korczak.html

Jones, Maggie. "The Smuggler Irena." *The New York Times*. 24 Dec. 2008. 29 July 2010. www.nytimes.com/2008/12/28/magazine/28sendler-t.html?_r=1

Thomas, Robert McG., Jr. "Alexander Z. Bielski, 83, A Guerrilla Fighter Who Harried Nazis and Saved Jews, Is Dead." *The New York Times*. 23 Aug. 1995. 29 July 2010. www.nytimes.com/1995/08/23/obituaries/alexander-z-bielski-83-guerrilla-fighter-who-harried-nazis-saved-jews-dead.html?pagewanted=1

United States Holocaust Memorial Museum. "Aron (Derecynski) Derman." *Holocaust Encyclopedia*. 29 July 2010. www.ushmm.org/wlc/en/media_oi.php?MediaId=4000

United States Holocaust Memorial Museum. "Le Chambon-sur-Lignon." *Holocaust Encyclopedia*. 29 July 2010. www.ushmm.org/wlc/en/article.php?ModuleId=10007518

University of Southern California Shoah Foundation Institute. "Johtje Vos, Rescuer: Choices of Courage." 29 July 2010. http://college.usc.edu/vhi/education/livinghistories/lesson.php?nid=717

Zapruder, Alexandra, ed. *Salvaged Pages: Young Writers' Diaries of the Holocaust*. New Haven, Conn.: Yale University Press, 2002.

Source Notes

Chapter 1: Elie Wiesel. Nobel Lecture. 11 Dec. 1986. 9 Aug. 2010.
http://nobelprize.org/nobel_prizes/peace/laureates/1986/wiesel-
lecture.html

Chapter 2: Holocaust Education & Archive Research Team. "Oskar
Schindler." 29 July 2010. www.holocaustresearchproject.org/
survivor/schindler.html

Chapter 3: United States Holocaust Memorial Museum. "Aron
(Derecynski) Derman." *Holocaust Encyclopedia*. 29 July 2010.
www.ushmm.org/wlc/en/media_oi.php?MediaId=4000

Chapter 4: University of Southern California Shoah Foundation
Institute. "Johtje Vos, Rescuer: Choices of Courage." 29 July
2010. college.usc.edu/vhi/education/livinghistories/lesson.
php?nid=717

Chapter 5: United States Holocaust Memorial Museum. "Le
Chambon-sur-Lignon." *Holocaust Encyclopedia*. 29 July 2010.
www.ushmm.org/wlc/en/article.php?ModuleId=10007518

Chapter 6: Holocaust Education & Archive Research Team. "Oskar
Schindler." 29 July 2010. www.holocaustresearchproject.org/
survivor/schindler.html

About the Author

Rebecca Love Fishkin has written for newspapers,
magazines, and websites, as well as books for young
readers. She has managed an early literacy program
and worked in the communications department
of an international nonprofit organization that
repairs children's cleft lips and palates. She lives in
Lawrenceville, New Jersey.

Index